zendoodle coloring

Magical Mermaid Kitties

Other great books in the series

zendoodle coloring

zendoodle coloring

Magical Mermaid Kitties

Mythical Sea-Cats to Color and Display

illustrations by
Deborah Muller

ST. MARTIN'S GRIFFIN
NEW YORK

www.stmartins.com

ISBN 978-1-250-14156-9 (trade paperback)

Our books may be purchased in bulk for promotional, educational,
or business use. Please contact your local bookseller or the Macmillan
Corporate and Premium Sales Department at 1-800-221-7945,
extension 5442, or by e-mail at MacmillanSpecialMarkets@macmillan.com.

First Edition: August 2017

10 9 8 7 6 5 4 3 2 1